10 Ways to Make Money with Kindle Direct Publishing

Deepak Yadav

ISBN 978-93-5667-077-8
© Deepak Yadav 2022
Published in India 2022 by Pencil

A brand of
One Point Six Technologies Pvt. Ltd.
123, Building J2, Shram Seva Premises,
Wadala Truck Terminal, Wadala (E)
Mumbai 400037, Maharashtra, INDIA
E connect@thepencilapp.com
W www.thepencilapp.com

DISCLAIMER: *The opinions expressed in this book are those of the authors and do not purport to reflect the views of the Publisher.*

Author biography

I am an infopreneur and i make money online.

I have seen many ups and downs in my life.

But the year 2016 was the worst time of my life because at this time I was very much troubled by depression and anxiety.

I made every effort to get out of this mental state.

Today I am far away from depression and anxiety.

In fact my life changed after the depression.

I learned many life lessons during this time and I want to teach this lesson to you through my books.

I hope you get to learn a lot from my books which might change your career and life.

CONTENTS

Introduction

As the world is progressing, new opportunities to earn money are also emerging.

You cannot say that you did not get a chance to earn money because in this digital world there are hidden opportunities to earn money at every step.

What is needed here is just passion and skill, which once you recognize it, then everything will be according to you.

I am fond of writing but I did not get such an opportunity to present this art to the world.

Will today's world believe on such an excuse?

No way.

Because today every person has come to know that through digital marketing there is no such work which is not possible.

If you look around you, you will come to know that today we are surrounded by digital things from all sides.

In this world of mobile phones and computers, everything has become digital, even books.

Whenever you want, online or offline, you can read books related to the subject of your choice and not only this, if you want, you can write a book and self-publish it.

You will be surprised to know this, but this thing is as true as it is that now you can earn money by working from home.

If you want, you can present the art of your writing in front of people and earn money from it, for which today the Internet is providing all kinds of facilities.

One of these facilities is Amazon Kindle Direct Publishing.

This is a platform where you can publish any book written by you and earn money by doing many things which we are going to talk about next.

This is a very popular platform, which if used for the right works can earn up to lakhs of rupees a month.

Here you are able to work by taking time out of your own free will and it gives you every opportunity of progress.

So without wasting time, first of all let us know what is Kindle Direct Publishing and what are the necessary steps we have to take to use it.

What is the Kindle direct Publishing?
Kindle Direct Publishing is the feature of Amazon where you can publish your books.

It was started by Amazon in 2007 and was known as Digital Text Platform.

By launching this, Amazon's company has given a career option for those people who have the art of writing and want to progress with this art.

Kindle Direct Publishing is a platform where people get the freedom that they can earn profit by publishing their books independently.

If you want to adopt the profession of writing or want to publish a book, then with the help of this platform you can easily do this work.

You can see that there are many such platforms on social media or internet, where you can do this kind of work i.e. online publishing work, but in those platforms, the matter becomes a bit complicated because all the facilities you get in Kindle Direct Publishing platform. That facility is not available in other platforms.

Those who work in this profession will definitely agree with us that after preparing a book, the biggest problem is where to publish it, then the answer to this question is - Kindle Direct Publishing.

By publishing your book here, you can reach out to millions of people and hone your skills.

To use Amazon Kindle Direct Publishing, 4 things are required, the first being to create an account on Amazon, a bank account, a book written by you and patience as well as skill and passion.

If all these things are available with you then you are absolutely ready to publish your book and you will not face any kind of obstruction here.

But there is also a question here whether money is earned only by publishing books on this platform?

No.

You can earn money in many other ways on this platform.

Here you will find such ways by which you can get more profit with less effort.

Do you know that with the help of the tools available in Amazon, handwriting can be prepared and you can also make the cover of your book from here.

If the quality of your book is good and you have prepared a book on a great topic, then you will not have to face any kind of problem because the best quality items may take time to come in front of the world but She definitely comes forward.

That's why your e-book will definitely come in front of people and they will also like it.

Whenever people hear about Amazon KDP ie Kindle Direct Publishing, the first thing that comes to their mind is that what is KDP and how it can be used and how to earn money?

And looking at these questions, we have brought all the information related to it for you so that you will easily understand what is KDP and how it can be used.

As you have already known that KDP is a service of Amazon's company which is used for works like book publishing.

But there are still some questions that must be arising in your mind like how can amazon kdp be used? And what are the benefits that can be taken from here?

That's why we have tried our best that you get all the information related to it from beginning to end.

So let us know how KDP is used and what are the necessary tasks to use KDP?

So let us tell you that first you have to register on KDP, only then you will be able to take advantage of it, but now the question arises that how to register?

You will also get the answer to this question in further detail, so read the following information carefully so that you do not have to face any kind of trouble-

How to Register on Kindle Direct Publishing?
Creating an account on Kindle Direct Publishing is very easy and to make it even easier, we are going to tell you in very simple words how to register on Kindle Direct Publishing.

So follow the steps given below and finally your Kindle Direct Publishing account will be ready-

First you have to go to the website of Amazon Kindle Direct Publishing.

When you will visit this website you will see that you will see the option of sign up where you have to click.

After clicking on it, a page will open in front of you in which a form will appear where many information will be asked from you.

You have to fill this form where you will have to give details like name, email id, password etc.

After this you have to click on Create Your KDP Account and as soon as you click on it, an OTP will come in your email id which you will have to register.

After entering the OTP, a new page will open in front of you in which the policy of Amazon KDP will be written.

Here you have to read their policy carefully and accept it.

After this, the dashboard of Amazon Kindle Direct Publishing will open in front of you and when you click on the dashboard, first you will have to complete your profile and to complete your profile you will have to click on the button of Update Now.

After this you will be asked to register the mobile number and once you register the mobile number again an OTP will be sent to your phone.

After filling that OTP, your mobile number will be verified and after the mobile number is verified, you will again come to the dashboard.

Here you will see that you will be asked to register publisher information, here you have to enter your country name, your name, your address, and mobile number.

You will see that there is also an option of getting pad in front of you, in which you have to fill your bank details and if you do not want to fill it in the beginning, then you can also skip it.

After this you will have to provide some tax information.

Now you will see that after providing all this information, your Amazon Kindle Direct Publishing account will be created and you can login to your Amazon Kindle Direct Publishing account whenever you want using your email id and password.

So that's how you see how easy it is to log in to the Amazon Kindle Direct publishing platform.

Those who had doubts about Kindle Direct Publishing, hope it has been cleared and you must have understood how to create an account here.

There will be many people who will still have the question that why Amazon KDP is the best for work like book publishing?

So let us tell them that there are many popular features inside KDP i.e. Amazon Kindle Direct Publishing, which has some advantages of its own, which gives us the facility to publish the book.

Let us tell you what are the benefits of Amazon Kindle Direct Publishing which make your work easy-

Benefits of Kindle Direct Publishing?
If you have ever heard the name of Amazon Kindle Direct Publishing or have seen its ads, then you must also know that this is a great way to publish a book.

It has many advantages like here you can publish your e book i.e. electronic book which can be read online or offline anytime in laptop and mobile.

Under this, such features are available to you that you can increase or decrease the price of your book at any time, that is, you can change its value.

Where you get royalty for e-book and paper back, in which your share in e-book is more than 70% and in paperback is more than 60%.

All the information about ebook and paper bag will also be told to you in detail here so that there will be no doubt in your mind regarding any subject.

The biggest and good thing about this platform is that this platform has reach to big countries like India, USA, Canada, UK, Germany, France Italy, Spain, Japan, Brazil, Mexico and Australia.

Therefore, if you use this platform for your book publication, then you can make business relations with the people there by spreading the name of your book to every corner of the world with very little investment.

There is no scope for any kind of mistakes here and the reason behind this is that Amazon company takes any kind of rights infringement very seriously.

Therefore, if you publish your book here, then it is very important that your book or any material does not violate the rights like policy, c, trademark set by them.

On Amazon Kindle Direct Publishing you can login anytime by creating an Amazon KDP account using your email ID and give your book in whatever format you want.

Here the work of publishing your book can be done easily, for which you get options like title, description, keywords, category and price here, which makes your account look even more professional.

So you saw that you get many such benefits under Kindle Direct Publishing which makes it different from the rest of the publishing platform.

But can more income be created by publishing books on this platform?

Do we have to work hard for Amazon Kindle Direct Publishing income?

Can I earn money by just publishing books here?

What are the ways in which money can be made using Kindle Direct Publishing?

Is publishing a book in Kindle Direct Publishing a good career option?

Many such questions must be coming in your mind, which is very important to get answers to and the purpose of this book is also that you get the right answers to all these questions here.

After knowing about all the benefits of Kindle Direct Publishing, your curiosity must have increased a lot to know how you can support yourself and your family by working on this platform.

So let's know what are the ways by which all the work becomes easy and you can start a new career in your career-

10 ways to make money in kindle direct publishing-

Here we have brought great ways to earn money from Kindle Direct Publishing, which you have hardly heard about before because many people consider it as a way to earn money just by publishing books.

Although it is true to some extent that money is earned by publishing a book here, but very few people know what to do under that book.

So if you are also curious to know about these methods and are looking for new career options, then this book is just for you, so let's start without delay how to earn money from Kindle Direct Publishing-

The main topic of this book is to earn money by publishing the book, so we have placed this method on the number one position in the top 10 methods.

Today every person finds it more convenient to read ebook because it can be read anywhere and anywhere.

As you know that ebook is a book to be read on mobile or computer and you can also read it offline, so it has become even more popular.

In view of this, many people have made their career and are earning up to lakhs of rupees by publishing ebooks.

If you also want to earn money by publishing Ebook, then you can publish your Ebook on Kindle Direct Publishing.

Publishing an e-book on Kindle Direct Publishing is very easy, let us know what you have to do for this-

First of all, you have to create your account on Amazon Kindle Direct Publishing and after creating account you have to follow the steps given below-

First of all, you have to login to your Amazon KDP account and go to the Dashboard.

Here you will see that you will get the e-book publish option, which is available in 3 parts, here in the first part you will see the title of your book, the name of the author and other information about the book.

In the second part, you will have to upload the script of your book which should be in the file of MS Word, only then you will be able to publish it with Kindle Direct Publishing.

After this you have to upload and create a cover page of your e-book. On Kindle Direct Publishing you get the facility that you can create a cover page from your website itself.

After this comes the third part in which you have to register the price of your book, select the price in which you want to sell your own book and then publish it.

If you want to make your e-book famous among more and more people, then you have to search and prepare a good quality e-book and also adopt those methods by which people can be attracted towards you.

For example, you have to make the cover page of your book attractive, after which people are forced to buy your book and you can get maximum profit.

Kindle Direct Publishing is a very good way for those who want to advance their career through writing.

It is very easy to use all the features here, so there is no problem in publishing the book here.

Also, here you can publish the book absolutely free, so it is an even more popular platform.

There is only one condition for publishing the book here and that is that your e-book is written on MS Word and follows all the policies of Kindle Direct Publishing, after that you can easily publish your e-book by creating an account on this platform. Can and sell.

By publishing paperback or hardcover

You must know about paper back and hard cover, but have you ever heard that you can earn money by publishing paperback or hard cover.

Before knowing how to earn money by publishing paper back and hard cover, let us know what is paperback and hard cover?

A paper back is a thin cardboard or paper cover book that can be easily folded and taken anywhere.

When you create a paper back on Kindle Direct Publishing and want to sell it, you have to format two types of files, a menu script file, which contains the outline of your book, that is, it is the inside part of your book. and includes the front matter, body matter and back matter and the other is the cover file which is the outside part of it.

In this way a book is made by combining the front, back and interior.

Kindle Direct Publishing has all the facilities of uploading both the files by format, so if you prepare and publish paper bags, then you can earn a lot of money from that too.

Under it you can also set the trim size and margins, and if you have visual elements that cover the end of the page, you can set the interior file of your paperback with a bleed.

You can also set the front page, body and back matter elements like title, copyright, chapter and heading etc. After that save and upload your interior file.

Also, here you can download the template for paperback and format your cover file, this is how the paper bag is prepared.

In those who visit Kindle Direct Publishing, whoever likes your paper back will definitely buy them.

After this comes the hard cover, if we talk about the difference between hard cover and paperback, then where paperback is lightweight, compact and easily transportable, the hard cover is stronger and more attractive than paper bags.

The quality of hard cover is better than paper bag, so people prefer to read it more, so if you publish by making a hard cover, then the chances of selling it are more.

People buy hard cover or paperback according to their budget because hard cover is made of cardboard and covered with cloth, plastic and leather so its value is more than paper bag so if you can make a good hard cover So by publishing it you can easily earn money.

With all the formatting tools available at Kindle Direct Publishing, creating a hard cover or paper bag is much easier and easier to publish.

Many people must be asking this question that if the value of paperback is less than hard cover then why are hard covers made?

So as you know the hard cover is made of a strong cardboard, so the publishers design them in such a way that they can protect it for a long time, so those who have to keep the books for a long time can use the hard cover book. buy.

If we talk about e-book, then if you make the cover of your book as a hard cover, then its quality starts to look even better because it attracts people, so it would be more beneficial to publish by making a hard cover instead of paperback. Is.

Those people who want to buy paperback or hard cover for their e-book, they can also buy paper back or hard cover published by you and this is what you get the most benefit because there are many people who have books ready. But they have trouble in preparing the cover, then they prefer to buy paperback or hard cover, in this way you can earn a lot of money through both cover pages.

By becoming a ghostwriter

Have you ever heard of ghostwriting?

Do you know what work you have to do under this?

If not, then let us tell you that ghostwriting is a great way to earn money as a freelancer.

Let us know what is ghostwriting and how it can be used inside Amazon Kindle Direct Publishing and earn money.

So the first question comes, what is a ghostwriter?

Under Ghostwriting, a writer writes articles, books, speeches, blocks, content, etc., for his client, for which he is not given any credit, that is, his work is only to prepare a project and give it to his client, on which only his client has the right. And in return for this work, the ghostwriter is given his payment.

You can simply understand that ghostwriting means working undercover means doing such work which you cannot present to the world with your name.

The ghostwriter just writes the project according to his client and takes money in return.

The demand for this type of work has become very high today because now people have started knowing that a lot of money can be earned by doing these works.

Suppose someone asks you to prepare an e-book and is ready to pay you a lot of money in return, then you prepare and give this book to him, which your client can publish anywhere in his name. So the work you did is ghostwriting.

Now it comes to how ghostwriting can be done on Kindle Direct Publishing?

Amazon Kindle Direct Publishing is a medium for publishing e-books where many people publish their books, so if you want, you can take a project from any client and create an e-book for them, which your client will publish on Kindle Direct Publishing. And then in return you will be given money according to your e-book.

How are there many people who publish books written by others on Amazon Kindle Direct Publishing and earn a lot of money from them, so if you do not want to publish your own e-book then you can become a ghostwriter for someone else. You can prepare a book and earn money.

Many people must be asking this question that if you can create an e-book yourself, then why should you do ghostwriting work for someone else when you can publish your own book and earn more money.

So let us tell you that there are many benefits to ghostwriting such as the first advantage you know is that you will prepare a book for someone else and you will get money in return for it.

The second advantage is that you can take charge of creating an e-book as per your requirement and this task also depends on the project assigned to you.

The bigger the project, the more money you can charge.

There is also an advantage of doing this work that if you are new in this field, then you will get experience while doing this work, after which you will be able to make an identity of yourself in this field and after getting a lot of knowledge, you You can publish your own book.

In this way, ghost writing is also a good way to earn money, which is in high demand and many people are also associated with this field, so if you want to earn money by using your creativity for someone else, then ghostwriter work. It's a good way to do it.

By publishing stories

Can I earn money by writing a story?

Such questions must have come in the mind of many people, then the answer is yes, you can earn a lot of money by writing a story.

But the question comes how?

So the answer is Kindle Direct Publishing which is a popular service of Amazon.

There are many such people who write stories from the comfort of their homes and are earning a lot of money by publishing them.

If you also want to become one of them then feel free to make your career in this field.

You will find many such people who are fond of reading stories, although every person's preference is different, some like suspense stories, some like thrillers, some like horror stories and some people have inspiration. But even today many people are fond of stories and you can take advantage of this and earn a lot of money.

If you have a good knowledge of a subject and you can present a good story on it, then you can benefit a lot by using this art of yours.

There are very few people who have the talent to write stories and they are able to attract people with their stories, so if you think that this talent is hidden in you, then through Kindle Direct Publishing, you can make this art of yours. can present to the world.

The best thing here is that you can write your stories in any language whether it is in Hindi or in English or in any other language.

If you think that there are people around you who like Hindi stories, then you can publish by writing Hindi stories.

If you want, you can also write inspirational stories for children.

Whatever the topic is here, what matters is that your writing skills can attract the readers towards you.

You must have often seen in the website or any other platform that people write stories and publish them and seeing these, the question must have arisen in your mind whether money can really be earned by publishing stories.

So we have given you the answer to this question in this book.

You can publish and earn money through Kindle Direct Publishing by writing different categories of stories.

All you have to do is choose a topic according to your interest and show your talent on it, if people start liking your story then you can earn a lot of money sitting at home.

Do you want to know how much money you can earn by story writing?

So let us tell you that it completely depends on your work.

In the beginning, you can sell your stories at a low price and see how much people are liking those stories and if you feel that the stories written by you are attracting more people then you can with time. You can increase its price.

The more people are affected by your stories, the more you will earn, so there is no limit to earn money here.

By Publishing Comics

Articles, speeches, blocks, books and stories are not only popular in the art of writing, but comics have also made a good place in this field.

You must have heard about comics before that comics is a medium where you express your thinking through the combination of images and words, that is, by combining images and words, you create a medium that can express your thinking in a better way. can be presented to the public.

If we simply put, comics is an art of conveying an idea with the help of pictures.

Under comics, it is very important to take care that whatever you are thinking or want to express, it is mostly expressed through pictures and you do not have to write.

Make a comic book with the help of attractive illustrations and publish it because there are many people who mostly do not like to read and they understand what you want to say just by looking at the pictures.

What emotion do you want to convey and what message is hidden inside it, all these story pictures present.

You must have seen that the things which are written in comics books are depicted separately by making a shape like a balloon, but very few words are written in it, so if you have this art in you that you can give your thinking in the form of pictures to the people. If you can present it in front, you can also publish by writing a comic book.

Writing comic scripts is not a common practice.

There are many such people who have made their career in this field and many people are engaged in this work because they know that comic is a medium to be used for entertainment and its demand on the internet has increased tremendously.

Therefore, if you can prepare any comics related to comedy, suspense or any other subject, then it can prove to be very beneficial for you.

Very few people have this type of art. There are many who write stories, but it is a very difficult task to convey a story or a scene with the help of pictures.

Here you have to take care of every little thing, like seeing the picture, its feelings are revealed in front of the people, so if you have this art inside you then you can earn a lot of money by using this art.

We have a huge number of comic book lovers in India.

Comics are mostly written in humorous terms, that is, funny stories are presented through funny pictures, so these comics have got a lot of popularity.

With the help of illustrations, you can represent any kind of subject on a paper and earn a lot of money selling comic books online.

It requires a lot of hard work, so if you are ready to work hard, then this work is for you, then in this way you can create a lot of income by publishing comics on Kindle Direct Publishing.

writing a book description by becoming a copywriter

One way to earn money on Kindle Direct Publishing is by becoming a copywriter, but let's know a little about what a copywriter is.

Copywriting is a professional work in which the emphasis is on advertisements, that is, copywriting is the only way to promote a product, web content, blog post, etc. by creating an ad.

Suppose you want to promote a book, then you can promote it by writing a description of that book, this is the work of copywriter.

If you have good knowledge of SEO and can work with a new improvement on each book description, then you can earn money by becoming a copywriter through Kindle Direct Publishing.

Here you write a book description for people, in which you tell people about the book, how it can be beneficial for them and can be useful to them.

There are many people who look for copywriters to promote their books, who can prepare a good book description and give them, so in today's date working as a copywriter can prove to be very beneficial.

As the demand for e-books on the Internet is increasing, so is the copywriter work.

Writing a book description is not an easy task, in a book description, those things should be written which are mentioned inside the book, such as suppose if you are preparing an e-book about a company, then you should first write this in the book description. You have to tell what kind of work that company does and what information related to them you have written in this book.

When your book description is solid, that is, effective, then people are forced to read the entire book after reading the description, so book description plays a very important role in any e-book.

Although you can do book description work from anywhere, but on Kindle Direct Publishing, your chances of getting a client increase because it is the biggest platform for e-book publishing.

So if you publish book descriptions for people in Kindle Direct Publishing then you will be able to make profits in a better way.

Also, under copywriting, you have to show new creativity so that people can be attracted, if you write the same type of description in every book, then neither your handwriting improves nor it attracts people.

Simply put, it gets boring, so if you start the book description work, then you have to try new methods.

Apart from this, you can also do a task that by taking a project from someone, you can publish a description to promote his book, after which people buy your client's book and you can charge money according to every sale.

For example, if you have written a book description and after reading it someone is buying your client's book for thousand rupees, then you can take 100 rupees as your commission in it.

In this way, you can get commission on every sale and earn more profit, this is a very easy and professional way to earn money, which if you can do it well, then you will not lack work in it.

By publishing business or health tips

To start any business or to get information related to your health, sometimes someone needs a guide who can give them good advice and they can do their work in a better way.

Today's increasing use of technology has put a lot of options in front of people, which has made it very difficult to understand which business they should start and where to invest.

Many people face this type of problem and to find the solution to the problems, most of the business advisors are found who can give them good advice so that they can start their business.

In such a situation, if you publish business related tips by becoming a business advisor, then it can also become a good source of your income.

There are many types of people who come to Kindle Direct Publishing who want different categories of books.

There are also people here who read books to get information related to business, so if you have a good knowledge of business and you can give good advice to people on this, then by preparing an e-book for them, you can publish it. You can earn a lot of money.

On the other hand, if we talk about health advice, then in today's era who does not worry about health, every person has health problems at some point or the other.

Some are worried about their increasing weight, some are worried about their decreasing weight, some have low height and some other health related diseases.

So in such a situation, a health advisor may be needed to maintain your routine and for a better lifestyle.

When you publish a good health related advice and people like it, then the tips published by you become more popular and more and more people come to buy your book.

Therefore, working as a business advisor or health advisor can be a very good career option.

For this, you should have all the information related to the subject well.

You will see on the internet that many websites are available where you will get more than one business and health tips, but when you prepare these two topics in the form of a book, then there are chances of getting more popularity because people get a All kinds of information is available in the same place.

Meaning, under health tips, they will get all the health related information and under business, business related information will be found in one place and they will not need to go to different websites again and again and search, so on Kindle Direct Publishing. Publishing business advice and health advice can prove to be very beneficial.

It is not necessary that you can publish a 200 to 300 page tips book on Kindle Direct Publishing, you can publish whatever information you have on these topics by writing as much information.

Whether it is 10 pages or 100 pages, it absolutely depends on your information, just need to provide true and good information which can give right guidance to the people and prove beneficial for them, only then your book will reach more and more people. Will arrive.

Become a book translator

Translator work is one such freelancer work whose demand has become very high today.

Translating a book is very hard work, so many such people will be found on social media who provide such work.

On the same Kindle Direct Publishing, there are many such books which are translated from one language to another and published.

This shows that doing translation work can also prove to be very beneficial but for this it is necessary that you have knowledge of any one proper language like if you are expert in Hindi then you can translate English books into Hindi. Similarly, if you know English well then you can translate Hindi book or other language book into English.

Translation work is done so that his book is available in every language and he can earn maximum money. You can earn more here.

Language is an important means of connecting two people, because unless 2 people understand each other's language, the conversation between them cannot go ahead, similarly until a reader understands your language, then he will not read your publication. Cannot read the e-book, so it is important that your book is in their language to reach as many people as possible.

The advantage of having your book available in as many languages as possible is that residents of every region will be able to read and take advantage of your book.

Those who know this keep on taking out the vacancy of translator job on social media, so if you want to start the work of translator then you will not be short of work for it.

All you need is a good knowledge of a language so that you can do translation work without any mistake.

In this neither you will get any language limit nor earn, you can work on that language, whether it is Tamil, Malayalam, Hindi, English, Gujarati and Marathi, regardless of the language you have. Whatever the language, if you have good knowledge of any language, then you can translate the book of other language into your language.

Once you have gained a lot of experience of translator while working on Kindle Direct Publishing, then there are many multinational companies that provide job opportunities for translators, you can also work for them.

To become a good translator, where you should have knowledge of the language, you can also carry forward this work with the help of some research and communication skills.

Also, an important thing is that you should also be aware of the subject from which you are converting the language of the related book to another language so that you can avoid any kind of mistake.

Kindle Publishing gives you the opportunity to connect with new clients and earn money by converting one of their books into a different language.

So in this way you saw how Kindle Direct Publishing can be used and earn money even by doing translator work.

After having a good knowledge of the language, it will be easier for you to work as a translator, so you can work as a translator to advance your language knowledge.

From Kindle Unlimited

Amazon Kindle Direct Publishing is an important service, Kindle Unlimited, you must have heard its name before.

If you haven't heard, then let us tell you that there are many books available for free in Kindle Unlimited which can be read through subscription.

It can be called a virtual library.

Kindle Unlimited's service in Amazon Kindle Direct Publishing includes your e-book and from here you can earn.

There will be questions in the minds of many people that if people here can read books for free, then how will they earn from it?

So let us tell you that Kindle Unlimited is a subscription plan in which people read books by paying every month, so if you publish your book in Kindle Unlimited, then there you get a chance that people will read your book by taking a subscription.

So this is how you earn through Kindle Direct Unlimited.

People visit here because they do not have to pay separately for each book, once they make monthly payment, they can access many books and the e-book owner of the e-book they read. get benefit.

Also it is very easy to access Amazon Kindle Unlimited subscription through Amazon website, this subscription plan is free for 30 days after that Rs 169 has to be paid to the reader every month.

Now you must be wondering how to add eBooks to Kindle Unlimited, so this is a very easy way.

When you log in to your Kindle Direct Publishing account, your eBook will automatically be added to Kindle Unlimited where you receive a global fund and earn money from both Kindle Direct Publishing and Kindle Unlimited.

So you do not have to worry that your book will not be available for purchase.

The more people who become a part of this subscription, the more you will get the benefit.

With the launch of these services, Kindle Direct Publishing has gained even more popularity because people can read as many books as they want.

Here you get a share of KDP Select Global Fund from where you can earn a lot.

Do you know what's best about Kindle Unlimited?

The best thing here is that you can select the price for each page of your book, for this you first have to go to your bookshelf and there you go inside the Kindle eBook action menu next to each book by login to kdp select You have to click on the button on the side, here you will enter some information after which a window will open in front of you in which you can set the price of your book, so by taking advantage of this unlimited service of Kindle Direct Publishing, you can earn a lot of money. Is.

When people start liking your e-book, then they will definitely become a part of your subscription and you will earn.

So this is how Kindle Unlimited works and becomes your source of earning, there are many people who think that by including e-book in Kindle Unlimited, earning cannot be done because here people can read your book for free but If people like your eBook, then they will definitely read your book by subscribing and you will earn more.

By selling your Services through books
Book is the best way to promote any service, because here you include all the information related to your service.

What is the specialty of your service? How does she benefit people? And what is the way to reach it? You can give all this information in your book, so selling your service through the book can be a better way.

As you know that Kindle Direct Publishing is the biggest platform for reading e-books, so if you publish books on any of your services here by writing, explaining about it, then you can get this opportunity to get your book. By reading this, the customer wants to buy your service.

Let us understand it in more simple words-

Suppose you run a business in which you provide different types of services to people but your business is not running well due to which you are not able to earn profits, then you can make books as a means of promoting your business. Huh.

You can prepare a book and publish it by combining the features of your service, its benefits, how to get it and its price.

It is not necessary that you have to publish 100 pages of books, if all the information about your service is available in even 10 pages then you can publish it on Kindle Direct Publishing.

When people will buy service books and read them, some of them may want to buy your service as well, so it can be a source of double income for you.

First, you will be able to earn from the book by publishing your book and secondly, if the person reading that book likes your service, then you will be able to earn by selling your service.

It is important that your service attracts people in a unique way because unless people see something new in it, they will have no reason to buy your service.

If you are providing the same service to the people which is available everywhere, then it will not help you.

In your book, you have to tell some such things about your service which is different from other people only then people will show interest in buying your service.

Whatever your service is, you just have to take care that it is unique and makes people buy your service.

Kindle Direct Publishing is a very big platform and as we told you earlier, different types of people come here whose hobbies are different, someone is fond of reading stories, then someone is here to take business related tips as well. People also visit to buy services.

Provide all the accurate information about your service in your book and see how this method is beneficial in growing your business.

In this way, you can also sell your service through books and earn money.

So these were some easy ways to earn money through Amazon Kindle Direct Publishing Platform in which you can earn a lot through your skill and passion.

Very few people know how to earn with the help of books, so hopefully this book will give you a new direction.

Conclusion

Here you must have understood how much more reliable and profitable platform Kindle Direct Publishing is.

In this digital world, who does not want that all their work should be according to their mind and the platform they use for their work should be accessible all over the world.

In today's growing world, there is a competition to move forward in every field, but it progresses only where the work is best than the rest and for the best work, the best platform is also an essential component and here you will find a similar platform Kindle Direct. Got to know about publishing.

The art of writing is in very few people and many people do not see any scope in this field, but if you know the right way to do it, then you can generate income by making a good career in it.

In today's time, no one has so much time to go and buy the book of their choice and then take it from one place to another and it also costs more to buy books.

That's why people read things like books, articles, stories and comics online because they find it convenient because mobile is such a thing that a person is present at all times and he can enjoy books online.

Therefore, there are many opportunities for advancement in this field.

Here you have learned that whenever a person buys the content created by you, you get money which you can easily get, so getting paid easily is also a big advantage of Kindle Direct Publishing.

If you are also a writer, you also like to write stories, comics, advice etc. and you can adapt any topic in the best language, then believe that Kindle Direct Publishing is going to play an important role in fulfilling your dreams.

With very little effort, you can make a new identity by giving your thinking the form of books and you can earn money by publishing it yourself on Kindle Direct Publishing.

Often we have seen that many such problems come in the life of writers which affect their writing work such as lack of complete knowledge of publishing a book, lack of knowledge of the right place to publish a book, not having money and more. a lot.

To solve these problems, this Ebook has been prepared where you have got answers to all the questions and whatever doubts were in your mind has also been cleared.

The secret of success is to work hard from the very beginning and when you work hard in preparing a book, then you definitely get the result which Amazon Kindle Direct Publishing has made even easier.

If you have a small budget and you want to get better results with less investment, then we recommend that you publish your book on Kindle Direct Publishing and wait a little while thinking about better results.

The introduction of Amazon Kindle Direct Publishing has given many authors the results they want and many writers have made a mark in a great way by using their art in the right place.

Today those people are walking step by step with the world.

If you also want to become one of these people and want to progress through writing, then you must also try using Amazon Kindle Direct Publishing.

If you want to be aware of such interesting information and want to try new ways to earn money, then do not forget to read our Ebook.

Here it is explained in very simple words that when and how to use these methods and earn maximum profit.

For more such information, stay connected with us continuously because we will continue to be present with new types of information for you.

www.ingramcontent.com/pod-product-compliance
Lightning Source LLC
La Vergne TN
LVHW041800190726
843493LV00008B/2726